Behind
CLOSED
Doors

Behind Closed Doors

Jamicka Lakeya

Copyright © 2018 Jamicka Lakeya

All rights reserved.

Paperback ISBN-13: 978-0-692-12851-0

Published by Jamicka Hankinson.

Cover Design by BrandItBeautifully.com

Edited by Naomi P. Washington, NewPaceWithin, LLC

No portion of this publication may be reproduced, stored in a retrieval system or transmitted in any form by any means electronic, mechanical, photocopying, recording, or any other-except for brief quotations in printed reviews, without the prior written permission of the author:

DEDICATION

Dedicated to my great grandmother

Glinning Hankinson

My grandmother

Betty Morris

My Friend

Harry (Skip) Butler

Thank you, and I love you!!

CONTENTS

	Acknowledgments	1
	Introduction	3
Door One	Love Affairs	5
Door Two	Fear...Of The Unknown	27
Door Three	Family Affair	39
Door Four	Breaking Free (Restoration/Healing)	51
	Afterword	67
	About the Author	69

ACKNOWLEDGMENTS

Thank you to the following individuals, without your contributions, this book would not be possible.

Thank you for purchasing my dream book. Thank you for taking the time out to read my work. Thank you for supporting me. I've wanted this since I was in middle school/high school. So thank you all for helping me make this happen.

Thank you to my coach/mentor Naomi Washington for challenging me, for helping me find my voice, for helping me in more ways than I could imagine. Thank you for helping me learn to say NO and for pushing fear out of the way. Thank you for helping me to understand how to be confident within myself. Thank you for being proud of me. Thank you for being there every step of the way and helping me get my book out. I honestly don't know how I could have done this without you.

Thanks to everyone who would sit and listen to me talk about my dream of publishing my poetry. Thank you for liking and sharing my posts on social media. Thank you to the ones that believed in me and help make this possible and for all the support.

I owe many thanks to my fabulous mother for allowing me to be so transparent and for supporting me, instilling so many things in me, helping me become the woman I am, and for being my best friend.

Lastly, thank you to my father for allowing me to share my truth and for allowing me to be so open. Thank you for understanding and making up for lost time and being willing to fix/work on our relationship.

Thank you to these awesome people: Antwan Jones, who did the artwork for my cover, Allison Denise, Toneisha Bush, Sierra Speaks, Annie Jackson, Tierra Cash, Angel Moss, Danielle Bush, and Montel Hughes.

INTRODUCTION

Behind these closed doors, you're going to find out so much and learn so much. It's going to be like we're the same person or I'm in your mind. You might think I know exactly what you're going through or what you've been experiencing.

Beware; this is extremely raw and real. POETRY IS TRUTH! I'm sharing with you things that I've been through and my experiences. Some things may tear you apart, and some things will make you smile and uplift you. You're going to experience many emotions, thoughts, questions, ideas, and everything in between. We're about to open (go through) many doors.

I hope that Behind Closed Doors will cause you to look, think, and see life differently through someone else's perspective and maybe even your own. Let the poetry in this book open doors for you and help you to know that you are not alone and can get through this. I hope that Behind Closed

Doors helps you to understand and learn more about **you**, your relationships, this world, the unknown, family, life, and healing.

So...let's get ready, and we're going to get through this together and finally reveal what's behind these closed doors.

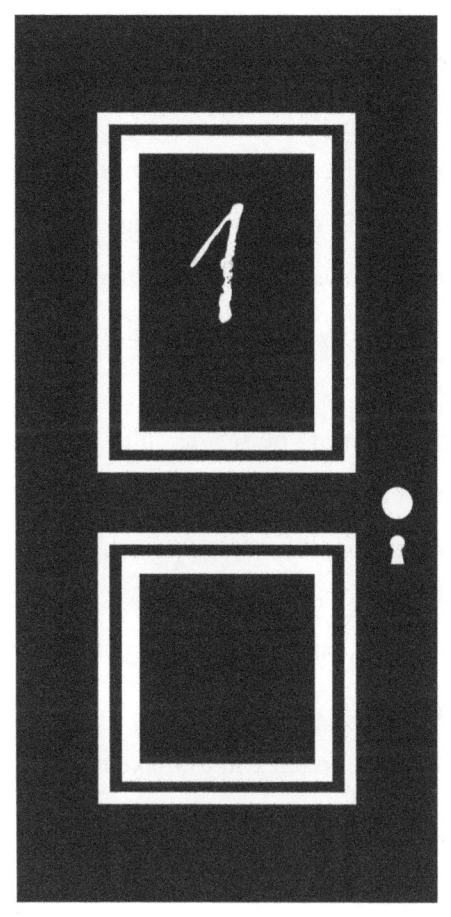

DOOR ONE

Love Affairs

MR. PERFECT

I have so much I want to say to you, yet I don't know how.

But then again, it's like we've been down this road before so, what's the point in saying something now?

I've let you get away with some many things..

You've lied to me, played me, used me and everything else in between.

What's the point of you saying, "I'm sorry, things will change, I'll do better"?

When in fact none of that happens but in reality I wish you would get your shit together.

You are old enough to know, and I shouldn't have to tell you how to treat me.

I shouldn't have to tell you to make time for me, pursue me, court me, or any of those things.

I stay and give you chance after chance because I love you and I want to be with you.

I've fallen so hard for you and the man that I see you have the potential to be too.

But if you wanted to be with me, your actions would match your words.

And we wouldn't have to have this conversation; none of this would have to recur.

Jamicka Lakeya

I care for you, and I love you, but at the same time, I'm beyond hurt too.

Because I shouldn't have to go through and feel this way with you.

MR. PERFECT 2

I honestly don't know what you want me to say.

You had me wishing on a star, praying for and over you, praying for us, believing you while you were out here telling me lies.

Thinking that I was going to be the one that you were going to be with and marry.

All the while you were out here living a double life, feeding lies to me, her, and whoever else.

And as hard as it is for me to do this because I wanted nothing more than to be with you.

I have to let it, and you go, I can't be what you need me to be anymore, I can't be that person.

Congrats on your new baby girl and family, by the way, I wish you nothing but the best.

I hope you show her the truth, get your act together and show her how she's supposed to be treated.

I hope and pray she doesn't meet a man like you, who'll lie to her and break her heart.

But if she does I hope it'll teach you a lesson because you'll have to be there to comfort her and pick up the pieces.

And then you'll know what I went through if she ever meets a man like you.

TIME AFTER TIME

I get hurt but then I turn around and try to love as I've never been hurt before.

Time after time again the same thing happens and nevertheless it always hurts more.

Someone gets married, someone ends up pregnant, or someone had a significant other from the beginning.

It's always something, and it seems like no matter how hard I try or how hard I love or how good of a girl I am, I can't seem to get that happy ending.

And when people ask how I'm feeling, I'm pissed and numb at the same time.

Because I've been down this road numerous of times and I blame myself because I should immediately have seen all the lies and signs.

KRYPTONITE

Why is that I let you have this hold on me?

It's like you're my drug and I'm your dope fiend.

I know deep down that you are no good for me.

But, I just can't let you go because we have so much chemistry and history.

Every time I think I'm done, I always find my way back.

Back to you, back in your arms, back in your trap.

I can't stand that I've let you become my only weakness.

The only thing I fall weak to and the only thing that knows all my secrets.

I honestly don't know when I'll leave or when enough will be enough.

When I'm no longer under your spell or yearning your touch

No matter how detrimental you are to me or how much strife you bring to my life…

I can't seem to let you go because you are my kryptonite.

THE TRUTH

The truth is yeah, I do think about you.

But then at certain times, I hate you too.

Sometimes I wished that you never exist.

And then at certain times, you're the one I miss.

Have you ever heard that actions speak louder than words?

Well, maybe I should act out my feelings and show you what you don't deserve.

The truth is yeah, I do care.

Even though to you, my feelings I can't share.

I can't stand to see your face.

With you in my heart, you'll never have that place.

I can't stand to see or hear about you anymore.

There is no longer an us, not a chance, not anymore.

The truth is I have mixed emotions when it comes to you.

The truth is I'm confused and don't know what to do.

HARD TO LET GO

I know what happened between us was such a long time ago.

But thoughts come in my head, and I can't let it go.

You both apologized, begged, and asked for forgiveness.

I forgave you, but I just couldn't put it to rest.

The heartache and pain won't leave my side.

When I'm alone, I feel a sudden urge to cry.

Two people, I loved for such a long time.

Betrayed me in such a way and now you're both nothing in my eyes.

I know I know, it was the past and such a long time ago.

But believe me, it's just so hard to let go.

HOT AND BOTHERED

The way you touch me gets me hot and bothered.

When you kiss me, I'm thinking does it stop here or will he go farther.

Take me by my hand and lead me to the room.

Take control, do whatever you want to do, but make sure it doesn't end too soon.

Savor each moment, relax, and take your time.

I love what you do to me and when our bodies intertwine when you kiss me from head to toe and go down south.

Then your tongue proceeds to slide up my body and enters my mouth.

Keep doing what you do, and baby don't stop because I love it when you get me all bothered and hot.

BREATHLESS

Some of the things you do to me take my breath away.

I love you and want you to make love to me every day.

Rubbing, touching, feeling your muscular, strong body up against mine.

Loving every moment of it, while our bodies are making sounds and signs.

When you are around me and touch me, I get all hot and bothered.

Especially when we're in bed, and your tongues glide farther and farther.

When I'm with you, things always get hot and intense.

I'm always thinking about you and you giving it to me every minute.

Lay me down gently and take off my clothes.

As our journey of lovemaking continues, let's do it, so no one knows.

CLIMAX

The way you make me, and my body feel, I wish that I could explain it.

You have me so high off you I can't but help to think about it every minute.

The way you use your body, your mouth, and your tongue I simply adore.

Your love and your touch have me begging and yearning for more.

You play with me and tease me to make my anticipation build.

My temperature rises; I get hot and try to brace myself for the thrill.

You know how to please me and my body, and with you, there's no more I can ask especially when you're the only one who can get me to this climax.

HOW CAN YOU

How can you sit there and act like something that you're not?

How can you act like Mr. Perfect when you're just as messed up as the next person?

How can you show someone how they're supposed to be treated but then turn around and do the opposite?

How can you preach about chivalry and being a good man but don't live that lifestyle or practice it?

How can you say we're queens and deserved to be treated as such but don't treat us as such?

How can you say we should be open, honest, and real with each other but you're not?

How can you say you have a girlfriend/fiancé, but then you're out here flirting with everyone else and giving people false hope?

How can your actions not match your words?

How can you not practice what you preach?

How can you be such a hypocrite?

How can you?

YOU SAY YOU LOVE ME

You say you love me, but you cause me so much pain. You say you love me, but you call me outside of my name. You say you love me, but all you do is disrespect me. You say you love me, but you abuse me mentally, physically, and emotionally. You say you love me, but you make me feel beneath you. You say you love me, but you walk all over me and treat me like I mean nothing to you. You say you love me but do everything in your power to control me, from the way I look to the way I dress, even the shoes on my feet. You say you love me, but nothing you do shows me you love me. I hate you, because this is not love, and this is not how love is supposed to be. But you still find yourself saying you love me.

IT HURTS (STOP)

It hurts, please stop leave me alone.

All I want you to do is let me go so I can go home.

Please take your hands from around my neck,

No, it doesn't turn me on, and no I don't want to have sex.

I told you no, and I meant what I said.

Get off of me, leave me alone, and please move from between my legs.

Put me down, don't bend me over on your couch and "hit it from the back."

No I don't want you to please me, no I'm not playing, and no I don't want it like that.

Stop, please, just let me go.

I'm on my knees and begging you so.

Please, stop it hurts so much.

Leave me alone; I don't want to feel your touch.

Please, please stop, you touching and hurting me I can't bear.

Stop trying to touch me and caress me everywhere.

Leave me alone and get off of me.

I'm begging and begging and begging you, please!

MY UNFORGOTTEN LOVE
Dedicated to: Harry Arthur Butler Jr. AKA Skip

The pain I felt when I got the news was indescribable.

I swear that day; I'll never forget.

You were telling me how you wanted to change your life around and did some things you may have regretted.

I was talking to you the day before, and the last words I told you was I love you, and I'm always here for you.

Never did I think one of my friends' lives would be taken.

Someone who I was very close to and someone I loved dearly.

You were my first love, my friend all the way back to Greendale Elementary school days.

No matter where life took us we always found our way back to one another and kept in touch.

I keep telling myself that this isn't real and the person they found wasn't you.

I look at my phone thinking you're going to text or call me.

It always hits close to home, but I'd never thought it would hit home.

Now all I have left is pictures, letters, messages, and the memories.

I promise I won't ever forget you and you'll always have a special place in my heart.

I hope now that you're at peace and can finally rest.

I love you.

-Lakeya

BEFORE IT'S TOO LATE

I'm telling you now because once it's gone, you're going to miss it.

So, you better take advantage of it and appreciate it while it's there.

Do all that you can even the simplest things count.

Cherish the special ones and make them feel appreciated.

When they love you, love them back.

Give them all of your attention and try to put them first.

Spend as much time with them as possible.

Please don't take that person for granted.

Because when it's too late, you're going to realize what you had.

So, I'm trying to tell you because once it's gone, you're going to miss it.

…….. I know I do.

GONE

Sometimes I want to treat people the way that they treat me.

But I know deep down that's not how God intended for me to be.

I'm always the one reaching out, making sure they're ok, always at their beck and call.

But when I need someone to do those things for me no one is there at all.

THE ONE

All I want is one man who is not like the rest.

Someone who will love me through all the battles and tests.

A man who knows how to love me like Christ loved the church, pursue me, and court me.

One that will be honest with me and won't mess around and cheat.

To pray for and with me, to love me, all of me, flaws and all.

Be there for me and catch me when I fall.

To prove to me that my search has come to an end…

And my heart will be his and his to mend.

THE REAL ONE

I prayed day in and day out for God to send me a great man well potential husband.

And after my constant prayers, he sent me more than I could have asked for in the form of a man.

This man was intelligent, well put together, a gentleman, and showed me chivalry wasn't dead.

I'm trying to tell you God outdid himself with this one and made me reevaluate all the bad things I had said.

I'm talking good morning texts, messages, and calls throughout the day to tell me he was thinking of me, checking in or wishing me a great day.

Making plans, opening doors, buying gifts, and paying attention to everything I had to say.

I was on cloud nine and loving everything about this in every form and way.

This man listened to me and supported all of my goals and dreams.

He vented to me, had big plans, dreams, goals, and wasn't lowkey about his feelings, and told me everything.

He put me and my feelings first and made sure that my spirit was well taken care of.

He even went as far as watching my favorite TV shows with me to show his love.

He was everything that I could have asked for and even a little bit more.

He did everything that I could have imagined, but I was still a little unsure.

See he wanted a relationship but I was cool with being just friends.

Even though he was perfect I couldn't commit to being someone's girlfriend right then because I was stuck on someone I shouldn't have been.

Behind Closed Doors

DOOR TWO

Fear...Of The Unknown

BECAUSE OF YOU

Why do I let you get the best of me?

Why do I let you affect my thoughts and my actions?

Why do I let you win and always get under my skin?

Why do you have so much control over my life?

Because of you, I've pushed my goals and dreams to the side.

Because of you, I'm always watching my back and worried about what people think of me.

Because of you, I'm continually trying to please everyone else.

Because of you, I've given up so many times.

Because of you, I haven't been able to be the real me, the me that God has destined me to be.

It's all because of you.

PANIC

It's dark; the room is spinning.

The walls are caving in.

My palms are sweaty.

My hands are shaking.

My body is trembling.

I'm losing my breath.

I can't breathe.

My legs are quivering

My knees are buckling.

I'm starting to lose it.

I can't contain myself.

Everything is slowly starting to fade to black.

This is it…

!!!

WORTH IT

There were times when I didn't have it all together.

When I thought having a baby or cutting my wrist would make it all better.

All I wanted was someone to love me or something to take the pain away,

To make my worse days my best days and make my presence worth the stay.

ALONE

In a room full of people and I still feel alone.

It's like no one is there, and I'm in this on my own.

Putting on my best poker face to make it seem like everything's okay.

When in actuality my mind is in overdrive, and I want to get away.

ME, MYSELF AND I

When I'm alone, and there's no one nearby.

No shoulder to cry on, it's just me, myself, and I.

Dreaming off into space and thinking how and why.

How is this happening, how am I alone, it's just me, myself, and I.

Thinking to myself why, and it never becomes clear, I start to cry.

Because I am alone and no one is by my side, and it's just me, myself, and I.

How could this be, I keep telling myself, dry your tears, wipe your eyes, don't cry.

No one in this world knows what I'm going through; I'm by myself, all alone, just me, myself, and I.

UNKNOWN

Sometimes I feel like being left alone.

No one to bother me or know who I am so I can be unknown.

Go to a place where I can start fresh and new.

No stress to be worried about or no drama to be put into.

Me, myself, and I that's what I want it to be.

Alone, unknown, in a place so I can be happy.

STUCK

    Just writing down my emotions and the way that I feel, all that I have to say/write is coming from my heart and is more than real. Stuck in between a rock and a hard place and sometimes I don't want to move, because if I do, I feel as if someone close and special to me I might lose. It sucks when I don't know, all these thoughts and feelings in and out of my body/mind moving how a river flows. Confident that I want one thing then the next I'm just so confused, trying to convince myself that the next move will be my best move. Don't want to do the wrong things and make a mistake to end up being hurt all over again and going through another heartbreak.

FAÇADE

I'm tired of being something I'm not.

I'm tired of pretending everything is okay.

I'm tired of faking and being the person that you want me to be.

I'm tired of being your, "Ms. Goody Two Shoes."

I'm tired of making it seem like I have it all together.

I'm tired of hiding behind a mask.

I'm tired of not being able to let my hair down.

I'm tired of being suffocated.

I'm tired of putting on a front.

I'm tired of being afraid you'll judge me.

I'm tired of holding it all in.

I'm tired of acting, pretending, putting on, and faking.

I'm tired of not being the real me.

I'm tired of putting on a façade.

POINT OF VIEW

There are times when I don't know what to do. So many people are coming at me, wanting me to know/understand their point of view. Everywhere I go, turn, and even to take a look.

I don't know what to do, and it has me shaking. Don't get me wrong; I love to help you all. And I will always be there to catch you when you fall. But you can't always depend on me.

I can't be there all the time to solve problems and make you happy. No matter what advice is needed or problem, you're going through. It will be alright in the end because you know what's best for you and you don't need my point of view.

LETTING GO

I don't know why we all hang on to something that we're better off letting go.

It's like we're afraid to lose something that we don't have.

Some of us say we'd rather have something than nothing at all.

But to have half of it is harder than not having it at all.

AIN'T IT FUNNY

Ain't it funny how things in life change so quick and easy, how one minute you're happy and the next you're sad, things seem to go your way and then all of a sudden fall apart.

Ain't it funny how you go out and spend all this money when there are people out here living on the street, people who have no clothes, shelter, or food to eat, and people are out here throwing things away and wasting money.

Ain't it funny how we act like we can't help a single person when there are children out there without a family, innocent people who are getting shot, beaten, raped, and killed.

Ain't it funny how people ask for help and get overlooked, no one pays them any attention until it's too late.

Ain't it funny.

HATRED IN THIS WORLD

In the world today, there is so much more hatred.
People need to see that it is affecting us in every way.
Killing, shooting, all these innocent people dying.
Some of us in this world are sick of crying.
Politics, religion, and race are some of the signs.
But if you believe it, we are all one kind.
All these things are hurting so many, and no one sees.
　Why can't we love one another and be one big happy family?
　I pray and pray every day that all of this nonsense would could to an end in some way.

Behind Closed Doors

DOOR THREE

Family Affair

TIL THIS DAY
Dedicated to: Glinning Hankinson and Betty Morris

Till this day I still think of you.

Even though you've been gone so long and there's nothing I can do.

You eased out my life a long time ago.

It wasn't your fault because God wanted you so.

But I do miss you and wish you were here.

To catch me when I fall and stop me from shedding tears.

My best friend, my MUH, the one I'll always love.

But, I can see you're better now and watching me from above.

DEAR MAMA,

This letter is not to bash you or make you feel bad. I love you, and I thank you for giving me life and sacrificing so much for me. I am so glad that now I know what it feels like to have my mother as my best friend. Thank you for taking care of me, and showing me the way, I'll forever be grateful. Thank you for making sure I had everything I needed plus more. But there are some things I don't understand. Why didn't you tell me that you loved me? Why didn't you tell me that you were proud of me? Yeah, you did it on social media, but that wasn't the same. In some instances, when I needed you to have my back you didn't. I honestly just wanted you to be there and support me no matter what. You accused me of doing things I had no idea about. You accused me of having sex at a young age and being involved with men I didn't even know. You say you trusted me, but it was only to a certain extent. You believed everyone but me. From the outside looking in, everything was perfect. But, it's just some things that I'll never forget. At times you made it seem like I did everything wrong. But, you did teach me how to make it, how to be independent, and get it on my own, but you didn't teach me how to speak my mind or express my feelings. But thank you for allowing me to be myself and giving me freedom, and not keeping me sheltered. Thank you for being there for me as a young adult/adult. Thank you for showing us the world. And thank you for doing your best and raising a beautiful, intelligent, woman. I appreciate and love you.

MOTHER, FATHER

I had a mother that didn't tell me she loved me.

And a father that told me he loved me but never showed me.

Of course, my mother took care of me and my father would buy me things here and there.

But I knew that buying me things wasn't love or showing that you care.

As a child, I just needed both of my parents to be there for me.

I needed them to show me and tell me that they loved me.

I needed to know what love was and felt like so I wouldn't go looking for it in the wrong places.

Because of them I didn't know what love was and would find myself in the wrong spaces.

MY DAD

The one that's supposed to care for me

My Dad

The one that's supposed to protect me

My Dad

The one I wish I could talk to at night

My Dad

The one that I'm supposed to have father, daughter fights

My Dad

The one that should've paid me more attention

My Dad

But it seems like I'm not too important or never mentioned.

MY DAD
Part 2

I love my father so much

I don't know if he has a clue.

I wish I could feel his touch.

That's all I want him to do.

He doesn't pay me much attention.

I'm his daughter; I thought that he cared.

I guess since he has three others, I'm not mentioned.

All the laughter and memories we're supposed to share

Sometimes I wish that he would call

To say I'm proud of you, or I love you.

I wonder does he even care at all.

I JUST WANTED

I just wanted you to love me; I just wanted you to show me that you cared.

I just wanted you to be proud of me even when I didn't get that degree or job.

I just wanted you to be the man I looked up to, to be my first love.

I just wanted you to show me how I'm needed and supposed to be treated.

I just wanted you to be that male figure that I could look to for guidance.

I just wanted you to be that man that you are now, back in the past.

I just wanted you to do what you were supposed to do back then so you wouldn't have to make up for lost time.

I just wanted you to want me, to love me, and be proud of me.

I just wanted…. it's not just what I wanted; it's what I needed.

WHAT A MAN

I've put on this front for so long and acted like you've been this oh so great, supportive, and reliable man.

All you've done is tear me down and apart then leaving me to think I was less than.

Yes, you've had your moments where you would try to do the right thing and be there or help me out.

But then after you were done, you would always find a way to make me feel bad and tear me down.

I can admit there were other times when you would pull through.

But then again that would be after I had to beg you and listen to you tear me apart and tell me what I do and did wasn't good enough for you.

I've tried several times to push your ways and your demeaning words out of my mind and to the side.

To make excuses for you and the way you treat me, thinking you'll change and drop your pride.

I've tried to be that person that you wanted me to be.

But I can't live my life for you or try to make you happy because then I'll never be happy.

You've told me things that have crushed me, hurt my pride and spirit.

You told me that since I'm not doing what you want me

to do, I will never be or amount to shit.

So, thank you for not believing in me and supporting me as you should.

But know when this nothing turns into something, don't come and try to be that supportive and loving person that you should.

FAMILY

My family is important to me, and play a significant part in my life.

Even though we may argue, they may get on my nerves, or sometimes cause me so much strife.

At the end of the day I know they're going to be there no matter what and until the very end.

To pick me up when I'm down, to lend a helping hand, to support me, and always be there time and time again.

And when I say family, I mean close friends, sorority sisters, coworkers, and church members too.

The people who've been there helped me loved me and prayed for me too.

Don't get me wrong; sometimes things can go so wrong with the bad outweighing the good.

But honestly that's just life, and everything doesn't always go the way you think it should.

But I wouldn't have it any other way because after all the bad, all the arguments, and all the hard times.

My crazy family means the world to me, they make days better, and they're mine.

DOOR FOUR

Breaking Free

QUEEN

You are a queen, and you should be treated no less than that.

Don't let anyone disrespect you, mistreat you, or put you last.

Keep your head high and don't let anyone deter your focus.

Keep your crown in place and put your dreams and goals in motion.

Quit that job, take that trip, remove all the negativity, and walk away from anything that's bringing you down.

Do whatever makes you happy, it's your season, it's your time, you're allowed to readjust, reposition your crown.

Protect your own and don't come off your throne and be the best you that you can be.

Put yourself first, have fun, live your life and do it unapologetically.

KING

You are a strong, black and intelligent man, a king with so much value.

You are the most important piece so don't back down or ever let society lie to you.

Don't give up, keep making moves, and pursuing your dreams and goals.

Stand tall, stand your ground, and no matter what, don't ever let the pressure make you fold.

Don't let anyone dull your shine or convince you that you're not a king.

Know your worth, potential, purpose, and everything in between.

You are dope; destined for greatness, my king you are it.

You carry my burdens, you have my back, and there is nothing you lack or miss.

Don't let the world hold you back or try to keep you down.

Push through, hold on, stay strong, and continue to wear your crown.

You are a leader, you are loved, and you are important.

You hold power; the world is in your hands, you're a king, don't quit, you got this.

WOMAN

You are a beautiful, intelligent woman.

You're a queen with so much value.

Take the time to live your life, have fun, spend time with yourself, and find things that interest you.

Take care of your mind, your body, and your soul.

Travel the world, hang with your girlfriends, start a business, see what the world has to unfold.

Don't let anyone dull your shine or convince you that you're not a queen.

Know your worth, potential, purpose, and everything in between.

You're more than enough; you are loved, you are important.

You're phenomenal, you hold power, you're a queen, and you're worth it.

THIS TOO SHALL PASS

Escaping all the heartache and pain that has been brought to me.

Harming me, mentally, physically, and emotionally.

No longer putting up with all the strenuous situations, struggles, and fights.

Leaving it all behind me, starting over with a new vision in sight.

Learning from my mistakes, wrong from right, and even my past.

Now knowing that even this too shall pass.

CHANGE

It's time for a change, time for something new.

Leave the past in the past and wait for what the future has for you.

Move on to bigger, better, and happier things.

Look forward to tomorrow and see what it has to bring.

Don't dwindle in the past but look ahead of you.

Having faith and putting in the effort is all you have to do.

Changes are coming, look forward to it and what it has to bring,

Happy moments, new love, friends, and all sorts of things.

Things may go well; things may go bad.

But don't let it bring you down and get you thinking of the things in the past.

THINGS HAPPEN FOR A REASON

God knows the plans that he has for us, so some things in life were just meant to happen. I know it's such a cliché, but everything does happen for a reason. You can't ALWAYS fix things and make them better. Some things are just meant to be left untouched and broken. You can't always make things work out the way YOU want them to. Sometimes you have to let go, live life, and move on. You are not beneath anyone; you are not something to be walked on. You are a human being, someone's equal, a gift from God. Some people in your life are there for a season, and some are there for a lifetime. Believe it or not, they will have an impact on your life whether it be good or bad. But you can and will learn from that impact. Things happen for a reason, and you may not know the reason right away, and that's fine. But better you know now that everything happens for a reason.

TO EASE THE PAIN

The only medicines that you need to mend a broken heart and to ease the pain are Jesus and laughter. Laughing will take your mind off crying. Another medication that you can use is friends. Spending time with friends and laughing can take your mind off the pain that you are going through. Even though deep inside you are hurting and the pain may seem like it'll never go away, everything is going to be okay. Don't let the pain get the best of you or defeat you. Just remember you serve an almighty God who is always there with and for you. Don't let the little things stress you.

WHEN YOU

When you finally learn to let go of all the things that have been holding you back.

When you have the peace and happiness that you've been longing for

When you don't need anyone's approval or opinion to validate you

When you no longer let things or people get the best of you.

When you finally know who you are.

When it no longer hurts, and the pain is no more.

When it all becomes clear to you

That's when you know….

STRONGER

Alone was what I was afraid to be; I was that person who always had to have company.

I didn't like being alone or left by myself.

I would let all these negative thoughts get in my mind and affect my health.

I felt that having someone with me would help fill that void and help me feel complete.

But I was so blinded by fear, anxiety, and the dread of defeat.

It wasn't until no one was there and I had no one to depend on...

No one to call on, so I had no choice but to learn how to be ok with being alone.

I learned that no one could fill that feeling of emptiness but me.

I had to learn how to love myself, find me and peace within me.

Looking back, I'm so thankful for that day and time.

Because it has made me grow so much and I've learned how always to have a positive mind.

I've developed a better relationship with the Lord, have a positive mindset, and found happiness within me.

But most importantly, I've learned how to love me and know it's ok to be alone and in the presence of my own company.

BELIEVE

All you have to do is have faith and believe, and he'll be by your side.

No matter what you're going through, he'll be there.

Get on your knees and pray and I'm sure he'll answer your call.

If you do something wrong, it is alright, ask for his forgiveness.

It doesn't matter what the situation may be or what you've done in the past.

He'll always be watching over you and your every move.

Just believe, have faith, pray, and he'll be there whenever and wherever.

Always loving, caring, and watching over you.

BEST LIFE

Life isn't easy, and no one said that it would be.

You honestly have to take it one day at a time and learn to be happy.

Learn to embrace every moment, the good and the bad.

Learn from your mistakes, love one another, look forward to the future, live in the present, and learn from the past.

Take advantage of each day, each moment, and live it to the fullest.

Grab life by the horns and hold on tight, because these are times you don't want to miss.

Speak positivity and happiness over your life.

Turn up, have fun, and learn to live your best life.

THANK YOU

Thank you for making it easy for me to find my place of freedom.

Thank you for being a place where I can go to escape.

Thank you for taking my mind off of the things that have bothered me for so long.

Thank you for helping me find a way to ease the pain.

Thank you for making it so easy for me to speak my mind.

Thank you for helping me find the words to express myself.

Thank you for helping me become able to talk about the many difficult subjects.

Thank you for helping me find my voice and the voice of others.

POETRY!!!

AFTERWORD

Now you know my truth, and you know me just a little better.

I hope that Behind Closed Doors caused you to look, think, and see life differently through someone else's perspective and maybe even your own.

I hope these poems opened doors for you, brought out any emotions or feelings that you may have had, and helped you address whatever you are going through or feeling.

I wanted this book to be able to allow you to be taken away from whatever you had going on, even if it was just for a brief moment, and to help you understand that we all go through things and there's no need to keep things trapped inside or hidden behind closed doors.

Life is full of adventures, ups and downs, and mysteries; nobody said that it would be easy but know that you are not in this alone and when the time is right, it's time to come from Behind Closed Doors.

ABOUT THE AUTHOR

Jamicka Lakeya is a new poet. She has loved poetry and has been writing poetry since she was in middle school. Poetry is her outlet, her escape, her way of expressing herself, and makes her happy. She has always dreamt of writing her book and publishing her work.

She currently resides in Aiken SC. She has a Bachelors' degree in Business Administration, Healthcare Management from Lander University. She is a member of the renowned organization Alpha Kappa Alpha Sorority, Inc.

Jamicka is a poet who gets her inspiration from her personal life and everything she writes about she has experienced. She also gets her inspiration from what she witnesses others going through. She is real; she is the voice of reason; she inspires, motivates, and brings a better understanding of what women are going through or have been through. She loves to read, write, and spend time with her family and friends.

Contact Jamicka Lakeya
Facebook:
www.facebook.com/lakeya.hankinson.com

www.ingramcontent.com/pod-product-compliance
Lightning Source LLC
Chambersburg PA
CBHW020958090426
42736CB00010B/1366